THE HOLDING CENTRE

Harry Clifton was born in Dublin in 1952, but has travelled widely in Africa and Asia, as well as more recently in Europe. He won the Patrick Kavanagh award in 1981 and has been the recipient of fellowships in Germany, France, the United States and Australia.

He has published six collections of poems, including *The Desert Route: Selected Poems 1973-88* and *Night Train through the Brenner*, all from Gallery Press, with *The Desert Route* co-published by Bloodaxe Books in Britain. *On the Spine of Italy*, his prose study of an Abruzzese mountain community, was published by Macmillan in 1999. A collection of his short fiction, *Berkeley's Telephone*, appeared from Lilliput Press in 2000. His previous collection of poems, *Secular Eden: Paris Notebooks 1994-2004*, was published by Wake Forest University Press in 2007 and won the *Irish Times* Poetry Now Award. His latest titles are *The Winter Sleep of Captain Lemass* (2012), shortlisted for the *Irish Times* Poetry Now Award, and *The Holding Centre: Selected Poems 1974-2004* (2014), both published by Bloodaxe Books in Britain and Ireland and by Wake Forest University Press in the USA.

He has taught in Bremen and Bordeaux universities, as well as Trinity College and University College Dublin. He returned to Ireland in 2004. He was Ireland Professor of Poetry in 2010-13.

HARRY CLIFTON

THE HOLDING CENTRE

SELECTED POEMS 1974-2004

BLOODAXE BOOKS

ISBN: 978 1 85224 971 7

First published 2014
in Britain and Ireland by
Bloodaxe Books Ltd,
Highgreen,
Tarset,
Northumberland NE48 1RP,
and in North America
by Wake Forest University Press.

www.bloodaxebooks.com
For further information about Bloodaxe titles
please visit our website or write to
the above address for a catalogue.

Supported by
**ARTS COUNCIL
ENGLAND**

Cover design: Neil Astley & Pamela Robertson-Pearce.

Printed in Great Britain by Bell & Bain Limited, Glasgow, Scotland, on
acid-free paper sourced from mills with FSC chain of custody certification.

TEXTUAL NOTE

This edition includes poems selected from these previous books by Harry Clifton: *The Walls of Carthage* (1977), *The Office of the Salt Merchant* (1979), *Comparative Lives* (1982), and *The Liberal Cage* (1988), published in Ireland by the Gallery Press; from *The Desert Route* (1992), published in Ireland by the Gallery Press and in Britain by Bloodaxe Books; from *Night Train through the Brenner* (1994), published in Ireland by the Gallery Press; and from *Secular Eden: Paris Notebooks 1994-2004* (2007), published in the USA by Wake Forest University Press. It does not include any poems from Harry Clifton's later collection, *The Winter Sleep of Captain Lemass* (2012), published in Britain and Ireland by Bloodaxe Books and by Wake Forest University Press in the USA. Detailed acknowledgements for individual poems are given on page 143.

CONTENTS

6

Above the Clouds

There it is, like breaded snow,
The cloudfield, the deceiving ground
Of existence. Cities, nations
Founder beneath it. Nobody lands.
The plane and its shadow
Fly in tight formation

On a banked white sea
Of immensity. Wedding-flight,
Death-flight, into the eye of the sun,
The muzak-filled ionosphere
Of weightless words, cloud-lexicons,
Hot whiskey and cold beer....

You could rack it up, the balance
Owed to yourself. The price
Of heart failure, burnt-out talent,
Altitude sickness, alcohol highs –
And the music of the spheres
Vibrating in your ears.

1

Blue

One day, you wake
Conscious of blue space
In which a pure sun has been blazing
For hours, while innocent trees
Perfect themselves invisibly
Just outside.
                    Ethereal,
Neither near nor far,
The city is a grey rumour.

Summer crowds
Dream at the intersections, register
The blue boundlessness
Of morning with a look
Of vague pleasure.
                    A good day
For the painter of white lines
On cracked ground.

Your mind is plunged
In the wrong kind of work
Too deeply, when Mary disturbs you,
Brushing gently against you
With her body, courting recognition –
I am a woman.
                    Later,
You feign indifference
To lost opportunity.

Work dissolves
In legitimate failure. Returning
Across this morning's field, you notice,
Where something metal has happened,

A smell of mowing.
                        Afternoon
Blue glimpsed in a ditch,
Forgotten again.

Far at sea, the white regatta
In which your lost friend is a sailor
Catches breeze. You watch it,
Sprawled among warm rocks of the shoreline,
Calm as the bay at evening,
Listening in to yourself.
                        Time lulling
The innermost shore of perception,
Inlet of blue immensity.

Voices of children,
Tainted with obscenity,
Reach you; a man who is drunk
Attempts reconciliation
With a patient woman; the elderly
Proceed on crumbling terraces
Of summer.
                    Night falls
Lengthily, streaked with the blue
Of many mitigations.

Michael Praetorius

The needle sinks in the groove.
The circles diminish
Endlessly. Memory revolves
On a still centre, towards which I move,
Into which I will vanish,
Resolved.

Dead uncles
Will be there, and the medieval music
Of childhood will come back, an infinite circle
Repeating itself, a circle of peers –
Musicians, doctors of physics,
Engineers…

I will be once again
Their godchild, on a stairway
Into darkness, gazing behind his chair
At Lanczos the Jew, a ghost out of Hungary
Bartered from Eichmann's ovens
In Forty-three

To the neutral zone
Of Ireland…there will be tunes
A child might mock, but a wandering religious
Whistles to stay sane, records for us
In an age of war and ruin –
Michael Praetorius.

Somebody's hand will reach out
To write algebraic formulae
On my blank page, before I am sent away
Into darkness, disorder and doubt,
A child instructed to pray
Alone in the night,

On whom will depend
Some day, this weight of imagination
Lowering diamond needles into the heart
Of an absolute recall, connecting dead friends
With the living, consolidating
Memory into art.

The Family Bass

Big with silence,
This beautiful irrelevance
Called art, adopting the family bass
As its chosen instrument, bodying something forth,
Has come to pass,

Untimely, when everything else
Has gone to seed. Arthritis touches the hand
Of the sight-reader going blind
Who might have played it, and the masculine side
Drifts towards suicide,

Drowns itself first, in public affairs,
Appearances.... Like a woman whom childbearing
Never aged, the female shape is pawned,
Its curvatures shattered and steamed
And then redeemed,

And I hear it, sounding
The house out, after the pregnant pauses
Of so many years, when spirit came down in the world
To escape itself, in family and politics –
Lost causes.

Military Presence, Cobh 1899

Childhood. A door wide open, day or night
Without fear of trespass, as long as the tides
Gentled Her Majesty's Navy...why not forget
It was a time of many suicides?

Everything else being equal, you are a child
In a casual doorway, feeding naïve plums
To the suddenly orphaned...somebody's father files
Past into oblivion, pressganged, a Cherrybum

Bound for the colonies. Corpses are carted back
From the place below, dredged from a deepwater quay
To haunt imagination. All you lack
Is consciousness, judgement, the twentieth century.

Calf Love

In the Northern wilds
That summer, driving through
From Donegal to Derry,
I saw you,
Picked you up.

You were forty
If a day.... U.S. reporter,
New World soul, corrupted
By a literature
In decay.

Here was the river
Meeting the sea.... I was spoiled
By a prospect of the Foyle –
No one had ever
Clamped down on me.

Bodysearches,
Caged humans, the windows
Of Catholic churches
Meshed in steel,
Grey areas

I let myself into
And out of, like a zoo –
An innocent getting the feel
Of animal atmosphere,
Waiting for you.

Looking so old,
You reappeared
At nightfall, disappointed
With yourself,
All your trails gone cold

Among would-be
Provisionals, appointments
Leaving you on the shelf,
A woman misunderstood
But not in danger.

True, you stood me
Up '...it's demeaning,
I'd feel too much a stranger...'
Causing a scene
In the bedroom,

Forgiven
Next day...you allowed
Yourself to be driven
Back to where we came from,
Part of the way.

I dropped you off
Somewhere along the road
Into old age, continued,
Unsubdued –
Sighing with relief –

Across the divide
That summer, watersheds
High above sea-level,
Unclouded, in my own head,
By time or evil.

North Wall

Some men estimate their souls
At six red tractors, or a gross
Of skins on the backboard of a lorry that rolls
Along the quays. Their invoices

Drift and whisper under the bridge,
The black steel bridge that drones
With unending traffic. Some men's pledges
Go with the tides. Yet still the big ships moan,

The ladies of commerce, out in the river,
To be delivered of such tonnage
As makes the city prosper.
Candlewax, peppermint – some men manage,

Bending their backs, an actual weight.
Some sit, apprehensive, in the warehouses,
Counting the fleeces coming in, crate upon crate,
Head dizzy reckoning up the tares.

And what is bartered in exchange
Is passing through the same, under the eyes
Of headcounting bosses. Briefly it's strange
For the mild-eyed cattle – the whips and animal cries

Of drovers – as they cross an unpastoral road
In the nightly day of the docks.
Herd after herd, slipping in fellow-blood,
In terror of sheet metal that closes, locks

Behind them, while drovers oversee
The working of such doors, all down the Wall,
As give admittance to an estuary
Of counted things, accountable for all.

Blue Room

In off the street is this warm billiard room,
Blue with nicotine haze, loud with hubbub
Centring on lit baize. Adjudicating scoreboards
Mark the small-time gaming of the poor.

See the men who have no man-hours play,
Anaesthetising rancour in blue afternoons,
Billiard games that pay only chits,
Vicarious economics: but these are compulsives.

Shirtsleeved shadows, they edge the tables,
Claiming, arguing. A lit cue dips to the baize
And angles an impartial ball to a pocket.
A score, begun, at nought, consolidates.

Hands affidavit under hard table-light.
Five o'clock passes, half-five. Big-time avarice
Has paid off its losers. But these play on,
Who have no stake in that more loaded game.

Middle C

Little girl, breathlessly climbing
The steep stone stairs
Of a bankrupt building, finds she is in time.
There's somebody in there

Ahead of her, practising one white key
Again and again
On the piano, or a medley
Of broken strains

Perplexing the house.
What must the weightlifters think,
Who turned the ground floor into Hercules' Clubhouse?
They shifted the junk,

After the original chaos
Of Nineteen Sixty-eight,
And put in its place
Their dumbbells, their clangour that irritates

Miss Maddix, who meant
Her one white key
To be musical, paid the same rent
To the same absentee.

Office of the Salt Merchant

Once in a while
I have wished to see more than the head
Of that girl who smiles
Disembodied, behind blood-red

Service hatches.
I wanted her hands,
From which a visiting merchant detaches
Yellow invoices, to extend,

As if in kindness to myself,
Pale salt in graded rows
Of crucibles along the empty shelf
Of the sales window,

Where I might see the atmosphere change
Her anaemic samples
As I did before, and stay once more in the range
Of a common example.

Morning

First light steals
Across the metal roofs
In silence, reveals
You sleeping, me standing aloof

At the open door,
Anonymous as when I gave
What you sheltered me for
Last night, assuring myself I have

Everything, while you keep
Night's language in a dark place
In a rhythmic sleep
Suffusing your mystery face

From the inside.
Nor will I break
That sleep in you, confide
Who I was in the act of taking

Leave of you, but drop
Down five vertiginous floors
From the high silence
Of your room, to where the clanging doors

Give onto sun and courtyard
And the photographic eye
Of a caretaker, introducing himself
With goodbye.

Metempsychosis

How transfigured I must be,
Being dead, I'm not yet clear.
My soul pines, moping dolefully
About the hospital square.

Soul after pad-footed soul
On the lonely thoroughfare
I've seen abdicate former roles
Already; and I'm hardly here.

I ask – what's left of me
Queueing for bodily care
At an overworked dispensary
On old, evangelical stairs?

And something that I've become
Sees an aspirant in my stead,
So absent-spirited, glum,
Who keeps hitting his dog on the head

Though leashed. And I cannot help
But wonder what God intends,
That through each querulous yelp
I hear the voice of a friend.

The Walls of Carthage

Augustine, ended the priest,
Put it all too well.
Here am I, a priest
In my late forties, still

In the desert, still
Relativity's fool.
Wherever it is the will
Of *lycée*, college, school,

As here, God to conclude
From premises, I am sent
For lectures, *journées d'études*.
Oases of discontent,

Paris, Maynooth, Louvain,
Define my forty-year desert,
Home from home, terrain
Of groundless visions, assert

The same topography
As he, Augustine, mapped.
Godless in Carthage city,
A dialectician, trapped

In a waste of comparisons,
His speech is my speech, speech
Of failure, of a man
Old enough now to preach

Of a God he may never know
Under the sun – a mirage.
So, with Augustine I tell you,
Alexandria, Carthage,

We, in inferior reason,
Travel until we fall,
To compare, in a desert season,
The beauty of their walls.

2

The Desert Route

Exempted from living, abandoned
To some infinite fascination he has
With a gentle goat by a wall,
Here where the trade routes start

The idiot sits, clad in the cast-offs
Of a town full of tailors,
Unembarrassed
By any such thing as self.

Around him in chaos, preparations
For the desert...camels genuflecting
To necessity, loaded with iron bedsteads,
Struggling to rise; and donkeys

With lank, hopeless penises,
Jesuit eyes,
Marking time.
                    In time they all set out,
Like free beings, across a desert

He will never go through again, relieved
Of space and time
To be lost in. Doesn't even notice
How everything still moves outwards

To the same end...the camel trains,
The slow asphalting gangs
On the superhighway, laying down
Lines of purpose, almost merging

At times, almost parallel,
Except at the border, where a soldier
With three stripes, wishing himself elsewhere,
Is waving the landrovers on.

Latitude 5°N

A forest of background noises,
African classroom... Voices emerge from it,
Angry voices of children, whose names
I cannot decipher, demanding
Euclidean instruments, Oxford dictionaries,
Chair of native wood
For their growing fundaments. Answering,
Drowned in the din of a construction gang
Levelling ground outside, I repeat myself,
Beseeching silence.

Or again, the night
Of the open forum... A forest of background noises
Planting itself in the crowd
Of black contemporaries, filibustering
The maiden speeches of girls
With shouts from the assembly. The M.C. drops
His faulty megaphone, imploring
Silence, but a man with a powerful voice,
Denouncing Western culture,
Has the floor.

The Catholic father, drunk
And disillusioned...'Give us religious war
All over again – the privilege of suffering,
Comradeship and martyrdom.
Oppress us, like the church in Eastern Europe,
Where you can't postpone religion
The way we do,
Just to go on a weekend spree. Above all,
Keep us here in Africa. Never send us home
Where we have no meaning.'

Sitting in the jungle, engine ticking over,
Thinking all this... No forest of background noises
To distract me, no radio drummers
Nationalising the airwaves
For a blood revival. Nothing but silence
Five degrees from the equator –
Silence of growth, before growth
Proliferates into desires. And the agelessness
Of the man with no birth certificate,
Innocent of history.

Loneliness in the Tropics

No one coming home
From North, South, East or West
To the unlit aerodrome
Tonight.... So they can rest,

The black nightwatchmen,
Behind deserted transit shacks
And talk. They wave again
As I reach the end of the airfield. I walk back,

My mind full of empty spaces,
Billowing like a windsock
On a pole. Already this restlessness,
An hour old by the clock,

Is wearing off.... I can sleep it off
After German beer
At the village whorehouse, if they have enough –
I have been here a year.

Plague and Hospice

Constantly ajar, as if created
For the acts of mercy
God is said to work through
Every day, this is the service door
The Sisters use, crossing a yard
From mission to hospital,
Flooding stone steps with light
Since half past six, when African darkness
Wakens.
         Around the steps
Fat lepers, bloated with indulgence,
Mope for hours, the question-marks
In the conscience
Of Sister Philomena. *What if these*
Were phenomena of Christ?
Her heart whispers. A night-light burns
Along porches, where the people,
Black out-patients, sleep
Beside samples of themselves
In evil jars, dreaming of admittance
To the drip-feed
Of an under-staffed heaven.

All quiet. An empty moment.
Sister Phelim watches
In the yard, where trainee nurses
Splash inflammable blue
Into tillylamps, lights for a Bible play.
Illumined, the animal beauty
Of their bodies – trimming wild flames
In the darkness, fixing the glass
To votive intensity.

Half past seven –
Everything normal today.
Rehearsals for the play.
The Devil said *Hmm!* in an amusing way.
Two priests came through
From the interior, spreading rumours
Of an epidemic, preached about
Beautiful deaths. Insomnia, cassettes
For afternoon rest, while the cock in the garden
Crowed, crowed, crowed.
A stretcher passed down the road
To a desolate burial, one child following after –
Two thousand years since Christ
Was first betrayed... In his hands
A labourer's pick and shovel.
Prayers, goodnights.

The Niger Ferry

Detachment, suspended animation
Between two shores...The Niger ferry,
Its shallow draught supporting
Heatstruck dreamers, halfway across

Green shallows...Lovesick and free,
Myself at the handrail
Of an upper deck, looking down
At antediluvian

Tradesfolk, brute soldiers
Dozing in military vehicles,
Mammywagons being floated from nowhere
To nowhere....
                    Is it still not time

To take control again, to resume
Wheels and levers? The dandy crewmen
Talk beauty, and I go on
Considering my love life,

Travels in search of a Rubicon
Dividing, like this peaceful river,
Past from future.
                    It still approaches
(Thousands of miles away

In Northern Europe) that jungle shore
Inertia floats me towards...the future,
Organising itself
Into taxis, there by the slipway,

In the increasingly human
Faces of taximen... Beggars and salesmen
Of bogus watches I'll ignore,
Taximen never be in time for.

Government Quarters

Reading the Greeks, African statesmen divided
Between Athens and Sparta, as the draft constitution,
Riddled with typing errors, clauses elided
For the public executions,

Goes to print...I look up their sources
Along the malarial shelves
Of our house in the tropics – basic texts of courses
J and I are teaching, children ourselves.

The government electricity
Our memory units work by, switches itself on
At nightfall, and we play
Defunct McCartney and Lennon

Circa 1967. 'Nothing is real...'
Floats from J's bedroom, where Chinese philosophy,
Local Indian hemp, define an ethereal
Adolescent, hired for his Greekish sophistry

By an adolescent nation.
Innocent and sensual, blackskinned boys
Who ran away from home, for a white education,
Keep house for us, bartering joy

For rational knowledge. Every day
Their unselfconsciousness
Wakens, sweeping the topheavy shards away,
Clickbeetles dead on the floor. We are needed less.

Indian Sequence

1 *Magnetic and True North*

This is the region of clouds. Beyond lies Tibet
Across a closed frontier. Bedridden in a room
At eight thousand feet, I feel how cold it can get
Without a companion. These are the altitudes
Sexless monks inhabit, briefly met
In the streets of Darjeeling, down from their snowy wastes
Of contemplation. Here are no dying multitudes,
No hunger, no chaos – only a servile broom
Behind the door, and tea diluted to taste
For English residents, refugees during the war
Who stayed forever.
                Into this otherworldliness
History steams, like a Himalayan toy train,
With its *Times of India*, news of Madras and Cawnpore,
And its goldenhaired Western children, dope on the brain.

2 *Jalpaiguri Junction, May 1981*

Noon, and the air is shimmering with heat
Above a stillness of trains. In the First Class waiting room
Ecstasy reigns, an atmosphere replete
With meditation. Wives with distended wombs
Are dozing in chairs, while fans in the ceiling repeat
Hypnotic cycles unto the crack of doom....
A storm is expected, but now is the hour of sleep
And empty platforms. In the shadow of iron bridges,
The cool terrazzo of a tropical station,
Nothingness rests its chaingangs, the coolies and drudges
Of organised labour. Watch the minutes creep
On a silent clockface, here where the wealthy in white
Sit spiritualised, in some Gandhian levitation
Of reading and writing, above and beyond appetite.

3 *On Indian Trains*

Disoriented, travelling out of the night
In a lone compartment, sun dissolving the mystery
Of imagined whereabouts, I find myself in the sight
Of people, stations, a vision of history
Metal shutters disclose, where the living dead
On the platforms are going nowhere, begging bread.
Behind me the mountains, the cold railheads
In the Himalayas, where meditation
Fed on itself, and the compromised beauty,
The peace. I want to go on in the dark,
To sleep through chaos, at least to Calcutta Station
In the hands of stationmasters, Hindu clerks
More reconciled than I am, to their duty
In a disconnected wilderness, dharma without destination.

4 *Calcutta*

Classical frontage, hundreds of years out of date –
I seek a night's protection in this dream
Called the Great Eastern Hotel, where the servants wait
As white as ghosts in the lobby (a little desperate
For something real to happen) and the beggars teem
Outside. After the ancient corridors
And the hush of lifts, this lying alone
At the back of everything, watching stray fires
Of the homeless, medieval chaos
Of rickshaws in the streets.... An electric storm
Approaches with nightfall, pestilent and warm
With its power failure, and its dead telephone
By my head, unable to close eyes
On a dark subcontinent, sleep on the unknown.

I wake in darkness, hearing a sublimation
Of suffering into religion, as the muezzin calls
Across a starving city. Day about to break
And the buzzards, godlike, flap themselves awake
On telegraph poles. Below colonial walls
A watchman dozes, deaf to the invocation
Of Mohammedan dawn, and troops of the Islam state
With their bought loyalties, guard the escutcheoned gates
Of Government House. Already, within earshot,
Scrapings of pots, and the uncontrollable crying
Of children, as hypnotism and prayer
Dissolve into day. I won't see anyone dying
On the road to the airport, through an atmosphere
Of annus mirabilis, unofficial despair.

Monsoon Girl

In the airconditioned drone
Of a room we rent by the hour,
You go to the telephone
Lovely and naked, to put through a call
For drinks, or hire a car
To take us home.

Your nudity dapples the walls
With shadows, and splashes the mirrors
Like a vision, in the blue light
That bathes you, a pleasure-girl
On a lost planet, sincere
But only at night.

Outside, it will rain
For weeks, months on end....
We'll come here again
As we did before, where Chinese women,
Blank and inscrutable, attend
Nightly to our linen.

We'll come again
In drunkenness, for the child's play
Of lovemaking, or to part the rain
Like curtains of jet beads
And dream the rainy months away
On pampered beds

Where forgetfulness lies down
With executive power
After hours, in a tangle of legs
And juices, a world turned upside down,
And I feed on the lotus-flower
Of your delicate sex.

At three we'll be driven back
Through depths of Bangkok
Already tomorrow. There will be roads
Closed, and a dope squad
Flashing its query through windowglass,
Letting us pass....

There will be lights
In Chinatown, sampans on the river –
The poor starting early. Elsewhere the night
Will separate us, having seeded within you
Miscarriage of justice forever,
And the rain will continue.

The Seamstress

I have a seamstress, making a shirt for me
In sultry weather, in the months we are together.

She measures my shoulders with tape, I feel on my back
The cool of her wooden yardstick, and submit

To a temporary contract, binding me
To the new and the strange. Together we lose ourselves

Among shades of blue, the melancholy feast
A culture of silkworms creates, as Chinese tailors

Stand and wait. For me it's the stuff of dreams,
For her a labour of love.... In her house on stilts

Where women are still slaves, she sews the collarless
Garment of pure freedom I have asked for

When I leave, keeping only for herself
Dry tailor's chalk, and the diagram of a body.

Death of Thomas Merton

Losing altitude, you see below you the flames
Of the Tet Offensive, giving the lie to your visions
Of eastern mystics, like uncensored newsreel
In which the slaves of history are spreading the blame –
And so your mind records it, a sin of omission
In a mystic journal. Meanwhile the wheels
Descend for Bangkok, with one of the Catholic great,
In late October, Nineteen Sixty-eight.

A clean declaration. One a.m. and you're through
The bulletproof glass of security, like a conscience
Filtered through judgement, leaving behind
Temptations you were dead to, years ago –
Hippies frisked for heroin, women and incense
For the American soldiers. Only the life of the mind
You hide on your person – all the rest you can shed
Like a stale narcotic. Shortly, you'll be dead.

So wake before daylight, breakfast alone,
Remembering what you came for. Below you a river
Seeps out of Buddhist heartlands, not in meditation
But in commerce, irrigating zones
Of military fleshpots, where the barges deliver
Rice and Thai girls, and a drifting vegetation
Drags at the chains of destroyers moored in Bangkok –
And you wait to be chauffeured, at nine o'clock,

To the other side of the city….
                              Spiritual masters
Shrunken to skin and bone, await you in silence
On a neutral ground of Buddhas, golden and hollow,
Smiling from inner space, beyond disaster,

To an old complacency. Starving for non-violence
In saffron robes, their shavenheaded followers
Beg on the streets. From an airconditioned car
You can see them in passing, as cut off as you are –

Cut off from each other, disconnected by history
In Paris and Calcutta, linked alone by the airspace
Of a temporal pilgrimage. Diplomatic immunity,
This is your saving grace – to restore mystery
To a common weal, and resurrect from disgrace
The nonpolitical, kneeling in a unity
Of monk and lama, prayer-wheel, angelus-chime,
For the flash-photographers of *Life* and *Time*.

Judas has other betrayals. At your last supper
In a Hungarian restaurant, among friends in Bangkok,
It's left to the Chinese waiter to overprice you –
So unworldly. You can switch from corruption
Suddenly into wisdom, through an electric shock
Turning your hair white, resolving your crisis
Into anti-climax. But it leaves you dead,
With a powerline shortcircuited through your head.

A small embarrassment, for the United States –
Your motherhouse, Gethsemani, awaits
Its anti-hero. A gaggle of monks are released
To New Haven for the day, to identify and separate
Among the Vietnam dead, the maimed in crates
From an Air Force plane, this body of a priest
And holy fool, from beyond the international
Dateline, and the jungle war with the irrational.

The Holding Centre

(Mairut camp, Thailand, 1981)

Irresponsible, singing in barbed wire,
Breezes lighten the silence
Of an emptied camp. After the trial by fire
With its destitutes crowding in, from the violence

Of the jungle trails,
This pleasure, this forbidden ease,
Transfiguring grief into beauty, soldier's tales
Into fabulous legends of the deportees.

Somewhere a pounding of waves, a whisper of grasses,
Encouraging, after too many years,
Earth to be true to itself, in pure ecstasis.
Listen, the music of Khmers

Plucked on a single string, by a soul-survivor
Lonely for murdered connections
In the grave, anterior lives
Surviving through him, guilty, resurrected

From love and slavery –
One of the singers.... Spared by fate,
Only the pair of us left, inside these gates,
Ours is the prison that saves,

The holding centre, its contradictions
Collapsing upon themselves
Like history, its tragic wards and its kitchens
Cut from the canebrakes, dissolving

In stateless space
That frees us, somewhere between
The absolute kingdoms of justice and of grace
Where a birdsong intervenes.

3

Dag Hammarskjöld

You will never be good enough, Dag Hammarskjöld –
From across the years, from another life
I hear your Lutheran father, ageless, cold,
Condemning you to the world, without a wife
To distract you, in the white nights
Consciousness rules, where midnight sun makes bright
Your Stockholm office, life that never extends
Beyond the arctic circle of your professional friends.

The years go by, the city now is New York –
And there I see you, above the United Nations
On your cold podium, priest and clerk
About whom the ethical forces multiply,
And babels of simultaneous translation
In space that conscience clears, while the wish to die
Prepares, already, the sacrifice you foretold –
You will never be good enough, Dag Hammarskjöld.

Your table is empty, the dinner guests have gone –
Your bachelor suite, too classical for the blues,
Has only a chattering monkey on a chain
To keep you from loneliness…. Why not telephone
Korean fruitsellers, rent-boys below in the rain
To visit you in your pain? Or must you refuse,
With all New York around you, beauty and gold
For a voice that screams in sleep, and can't be controlled?

You will never be good enough, Dag Hammarskjöld –
Exhausted man, I read in your book of changes
Gethsemanes of sleepless transit lounges
In the small hours, the missions that failed
And left behind them everyday evil, good,

In the holding centres, innocent phials of blood
Being stacked like bullets, under refrigeration –
Awaiting their hour, like massacre or salvation

No one controls.... So fly home to your father
As long as you live, immaculately attired
For the state of grace you desired
Under alien skies, in a different weather
Than ours which radio silence disconnects
And plunges you out of, there when you least expect –
Relax, enjoy that journey, be consoled,
You will never be good enough, Dag Hammarskjöld.

Conversations by the Hudson

A world comes back to me
Years later, hearing it said
You have been disconnected
From the life-support machines
Of America, and are dead.

I hear you say 'Decide and live!'
As if it were only yesterday
And the traffic on Riverside Drive
Streams through the back of both our minds.
I want you to know, I got away

Into the great world, as you did –
Guardian angel, pioneer,
Ahead of me by twenty years,
A face in the New York crowd.
'Just like us' you point them out,

The madmen rifling trashcans
Down by the Hudson, on day-release,
'Capitalistic energies!'
Liberated, soul-destroyed
In the American void,

Are they all we amount to?
The lights on the Jersey side blink on –
As we to them, so they to us –
And at our backs, the night begins,
Desire, frustration, enterprise,

On Eighty-ninth and Amsterdam –
Streetgirls waiting, men on stoops,
South Koreans, skullcapped Jews,
Everyone lost in a home from home,
Everyone free to choose.

'Go back on this? Not now. Not ever.'
I hear you say, above the roar
Of traffic going nowhere
As your fiftieth year slides quietly by,
No louder than the river

Bearing its cold alluvium
Out of America, one dark flow –
The jewellery, the real estate,
The luck not given, only made
By the gambler's throw.

Euclid Avenue

(after Hart Crane)

The blazing stanchions and the corporate lights –
Manhattan over the bridge, from Brooklyn Heights –
Were energies like yours, without a home,
That would not be condensed inside a poem

But endlessly dispersed and went to work
For time and money, hovering over the masses
Like terrible angels.... Now, I stand in New York
And watch those energies sweat themselves out, like gases

Through a subway grille, to keep the derelicts warm
In a new depression. Or, at station bookstalls,
Calm at the eye of the electric storm
I drink your words, like prohibition alcohol

Capital hides from itself. On soundless trains
Through middle America, citizens fishing in creeks
That rise and flow nowhere, disappear again
In a private wilderness you were born to seek

And lose yourself in. But none of them will thank you –
They, nor the desolate children whom they raised
On a thousand streets called Euclid Avenue
For travelling inwards, damning with faint praise

The forces that they freed, to blast through gravity
Into a loveless, extraterrestrial space
Like night bus stations, galaxies of strays –
The sons and daughters of the human race.

The Angel

Jokes, the strength of whiskey
And the infectious mirth
Of public houses
Bring an angel to earth.

The men are like giants –
Magnanimous, a little outsized
To be categorised
But they can hold their pints.

I don't float in here often
From the threshold
Of oblivion, but once in a while
My nature softens

And I climb down
Immaculate walls of churches,
Abandon books, laboratories,
Bloodless researches

Into the absolute
And go for a night on the town –
In spite of myself,
Somehow, my oats get sown.

The very next day,
Suspended in abstraction
Between the in- and the out-tray,
Or bored to distraction

At some meeting, I remember
Morning blue as the first
Unconsciousness once woke into –
Incarnate, by the window,

A sparrow is singing, and godlike,
I am lending an ear
To existence....
                    Now, in the middle
Of sessions lasting years

Where order is preferred
To the innocence of animals
And the laughter of humanity
I might still put in a word.

The Waking Hour

Riddled with contradictions, the waking hour
Is upon us now, and everywhere about us
Morning, the sense of existence
And the three dimensions
Coming together, whitening pillows and walls.

And I float upwards, from my own depths,
With a woman beside me
Wondering, wondering am I real
Or an angel trapped in the glass of a bedside prayer
And have I come into her life, and will I stay there

With the other objects, nailed to the wall
Like permanence, or habit,
Achieving humanity, averaging out
Between sacred and profane, through the long attritions
Marriage and work ordain....

Deliver us, Lord, from the loss of intensity
Now, as on every day
Of heightened beginnings, that pass away
With the first word spoken, the earliest bird
To strike a false note

Or the city announcing itself
In klaxons and white noise, delivering
To our disembodied selves
Wherever we are, the temporal fruits
Of Eden, the past and future again.

Early Christians

Light a candle, put out gospel fare
And waive discrimination
Just for tonight…. We're up four flights of stairs
In attic space that floats over Dublin city
Like suspended animation
Or catharsis, from the absurdities
Of rent uncollected
And power disconnected.

Energies float here, heavens or hells,
But the slow purgatories
Of daily living you leave to everyone else –
To the men in all-night factories, as they sweat
Among spare parts and machinery
Down below, and the ruined levels to let,
And the curfewed world
Of a Catholic hostel for girls.

As midnight chimes, in the bells of seven churches
From Phibsboro to Dominic Street,
Explain these captured birds, asleep on their perches,
All your tailor's dummies, incomplete
As humanity itself, your Faustian researches
Marvellous and discreet,
In a workshop of beauty
High above power or duty.

Nobody dreams of us, no one knows we're here –
Yet the lights of their private altars
Fail all around us, leave us alone in the years,
As coffee laced with alcohol goes to our heads
And we eat the last bread, and watch our candle falter.

When we stop laughing, we can go to bed
With no other prayer
Than breathing and yellow hair.

Ecstatic girl, would the Virgin understand you
For whom lactation and tears
Were the only truth? I lie beside you and hear
Anxieties whisper around me, like pressurised water
On a third-floor landing –
But yours, who are nobody's daughter
And nobody's ghost,
Is the sleep of the just.

Through windows without glass, at a condemned height,
To the cries of scavengers in off the Dublin docks
We will sense the approach of light
Ahead of our brother, the ancient vendor of clocks
Who sleeps downstairs, and has so many dependents
And all the shadowy tenants
Of a made millionaire
Now living elsewhere.

But leave your loins ungirded, stay in the dark
And live in secret, like an early Christian
Waiting for Rome to collapse
While I drive brightening streets, to be first at work,
Administrator of hospitals and prisons –
And hundreds of years, perhaps,
Will pass in a day
I will serve and betray.

Vaucluse

Cognac, like a gold sun
Blazed in me, turning
The landscape inside out –
I had left the South
An hour ago, and the train
Through Arles, through Avignon,
Fed on electricity
Overhead, and quickened my mind
With infinite platforms, cypress trees,
Stone villages, the granaries
Of Provence, and I saw again
France, like a blue afternoon
Genius makes hay in, and drink improves –
The worked fields, the yellow sheaves
In shockwaves, perceived
And lit from within, by love.

By then, I suppose,
You had made your own connections,
My chance, eventual girl,
And half Marseille had closed
For the hot hours – the awnings of cafés
With nothingness in their shadows,
And the drink put away
For another day
Not ours....
                    I see, I remember
Coldly now, as I see ourselves
And the merchants from Africa, glozening
Liquor on the shelves
Of celebration, everyone dozing
In transmigratory dreams
Of heroin, garlic and cloves –

And how we got there, you and I,
By trade route or intuition, seems,
Like charts for sale on the Occident streets,
As fabulous, as obsolete
As a map of the known world.

But then again, how kind he was,
The dark *patron*...and it lasted,
That shot of cognac,
An hour, till the train
Occluded in grey rain
Above Lyons, and the Rhône valley
Darkened. I would carry
Your books, your winter clothes
Through stations, streets of Paris
To a cold repose
In the North. We would meet again
In months to come, and years,
Exchanging consciousness, reason and tears
Like beggars. Transfigured,
Not yet fallen from grace
I saw us, not as we are
But new in love, in the hallowed place
Of sources, the sacred fountains
Of Petrarch and René Char.

Eccles Street, Bloomsday 1982

One-sided, stripped of its ghosts,
The half that was left of Eccles Street
Stood empty, on that day of days
My own unconscious feet
Would carry me through
To a blind date, or a rendezvous.

Invisible pressure, invisible heat
Laid down the blue coordinates
Of an Hellenic city
From Phoenix Park to the Merrion Gates,
Where disconnected, at one remove
From wisdom or eternal love,

A million citizens worked, ate meals
Or dreamt a moment of Joyce,
And felt themselves wholly real,
The equals of fate, the masters of choice,
As I did too, on Eccles Street,
Before ever you and I could meet

In the larger scheme.... Coincidence
Ruled invisibly, the casual date
Upstaged by Greek infinities
Moving among us like common sense,
Imprisoning, setting me free
To dream and circumambulate

In a myth too young to be formed.
I would build it myself, from the ruined door
Of Bella Cohen's bawdy-house,
From other basements, other whores
Unbuttoning their blouses
Forever, while traffic swarmed

And the lights outside turned green and red
On shifting planes of reality –
And you, eternal student, read
Of Joyce in the National Library,
Or stood in the crowd, my love unseen,
At the unveiling in Stephen's Green.

An hour went by, on Eccles Sreet –
Two drunks, at ease in the Mater portals,
Swigged, and sang Republican songs.
I watched a line of taxis wait
And saw where real grass had sprung
Through mythic pavements, already immortal,

Green as life, and unresearched.
I had come, only that morning,
From Ringsend docks and Sandymount church,
Along the arc of odyssey,
With my invisible yearning
To break the circle, set myself free,

As you had yours, until one day,
In the prefigured city,
Where every step is a step of fate
And recognition comes only later,
We would meet, you and I,
Weigh anchor at last, and go away.

4

Exiles

In our own city, we are exiles –
Strangers, through the closed windows
Of taxis, staring
At the selves we never became.

How they crowd there, the familiar faces
At the intersections! For them too, the lights change
Like an illusion of freedom
As they disappear out of our lives.

Today Dublin, tomorrow Paris or Rome –
And the blur of cities
Is one City, simultaneous,
Eternal, from which we are exiled forever.

And I say to you 'Let us make a home
In ourselves, in each other…' as if streets
Or the statues of public men
Or all the doors we will never darken again

Are a vanished counterworld
To love, that throws us together
In the back seat of our own destiny
Where one dreams, and the other gives directions.

In Earthquake Country

Slow as a landscape, character forms
In front of us, through a window in the mountains
Looking inwards and outwards together
At lines of nature, sandstone weathering,
Rifts that open between us, rifts that dissolve,
Except for the seams in our faces
As we grow older.

Look north, at the Apennines,
Their old faultlines. Earthquake country –
Blind tectonic plates
Are shifting the ground beneath us,
Our Mediterranean floor. Forget villages
And forests of dwarf oak. Here, life
Roots itself in the inhuman.

A valley of soulmaking –
Where does it flow to? Glacial waters meet
Down there, where we cannot see them,
Roaring in our ears
All night, while we hold each other
In this cold planetarium of lights
That closes us in, the children of Galileo.

Do they see us, as we see ourselves,
The windows turning gold? Good night, dear heart,
And better luck than the dead
From Naples to Avezzano – histories, loves
Before our time, that the epicentres swallowed –
While faith that moves mountains
Tolls upvalley, in its fissured belltower.

The River

When I was angry, I went to the river –
New water on old stones, the patience of pools.
Let the will find its own pace
Said a voice inside me
I was learning to believe,

And the rest will take care of itself.
The fish were facing upstream, tiny trout
Suspended like souls, in their aqueous element.
I and my godlike shadow
Fell across them, and they disappeared.

All this happened deep in the mountains –
Anger, trout and shadow
With the river flowing through them.
Far away, invisible but imagined,
Was an ancient sea, where things would resolve themselves.

At the Grave of Silone

Lost in the fog at four thousand feet
When the lights come on, I can see them all,
The mountain villages, so small
A blind man feels his way about
Without a stick, and everyone overhears
Everyone else, as they quarrel and shout,
And still they are all alone –
And the places, the years,
Who redeems them? I think again
Of you, Ignazio Silone,
Ten years dead, a hundred miles to the south
On this freezing Apennine chain,
A body interred, forever looking out
On an endlessly fertile plain –

And how we had visited you, one day
When August blew the crops awake
And harvesters toiled, in the drained lake
Of human promise…. Skies were passing away
But nothing had changed on the ground.
Heat and apathy, everyday sound
In your natal village. Unsuccess
With its local dreamers, revving their motorbikes,
Punishing the slot machines.
Fontamara…it could have been
Aranyaprathet, or Ballaghaderreen.
Without knowing it, we had come to pray
At the shrine of ordinariness –
We, who were running away.

And look at us now, a man and woman
Dodging the Reaper, saving hay
In the high Abruzzo, our windowpanes

74

Rattled by cold and the sonic vibrations,
Extraterrestrial, superhuman,
Of half a dozen airforce planes
That shatter the peace.... Again night falls
On this village of limitations
We have come to. Invisible forces spray
Their 'Duce-Vinceremo' on our walls.
As your books say,
All of us dream, and stay in thrall
To the usual consolations.
Marriage. America. Going away.

I shut the window, bank the fire,
And pick up Plato on The Good.
The lumberjack, who gives us wood
For nothing, I see him across in the bar
Where a girl is slicing lemons, tidying shelves,
And shadows argue, the porkpie hats
Of failures home from Canada, playing skat
And fourhand poker. Metal crutches,
Phlegm – the man absurdity trails
Like a village dog.... If they saw themselves
For just one instant, as they are,
Heroic but misunderstood,
Their conversations would carry for miles
Like the sound of a shot.

Castelli, Cerqueto, cold San Giorgio
Float in the fog, red atmospheres
Connected to each other and to here
Where I link your fate with hers and mine,
Unconsciousness everywhere.... Fifty years ago
In exile, writing *Bread and Wine*
The War was coming. Now, below your shrine,
Memory tries to wake
Blind monuments to the Fascist dead,

Disheartened villages, men who cannot shake
The ant of toil from their Sunday clothes,
Slatternly women, old for their years,
The Christian cross, the Communist rose,
With the human word you said.

Taking the Waters

There are taps that flow, all day and all night,
From the depths of Europe,
Inexhaustible, taken for granted,

Slaking our casual thirsts
At a railway station
Heading south, or here in the Abruzzo

Bursting cold from an iron standpipe
While our blind mouths
Suck at essentials, straight from the water table.

Our health is too good, we are not pilgrims,
And the nineteenth century
Led to disaster. Aix and Baden Baden –

Where are they now, those ladies with the vapours
Sipping at glasses of hydrogen sulphide
Every morning, while the pumphouse piano played

And Russian radicals steamed and stewed
For hours in their sulphur tubs
Plugged in to the cathodes of Revolution?

Real cures, for imaginary ailments –
Diocletian's or Vespasian's.
History passes, only the waters remain,

Bubbling up, through their carbon sheets,
To the other side of catastrophe
Where we drink, at a forgotten source,

Though the old crust of Europe
Centuries deep, restored by a local merchant
Of poultry and greens, inscribing his name in Latin.

The Poet Sandro Penna, in Old Age

There are those who will leave this world
On a gun-carriage, draped in the flag of the state
Like my friend Montale,
Always so careful, always so astute,
So politically in the right,
With his place in the Senate, his Nobel Prize
Like a state of grace
This side, at least, of eternal night –

And there are those, like my old friend
Pasolini, his bloodied head
Kicked in by a male prostitute
In Ostia – it could so easily
Have been him and me! –
Splashed all over the Roman evening papers,
Coming, in public, to scandalous ends
In the underworld of the id –

And there is me,
Sandro Penna, turned seventy
Last summer, without votes of congratulation
Or unexpurgated editions
Of the sexual poems. A fancier of boys
All my life, I have been.
For this the critics call me 'The last of the Greeks,
The most ancient of men....'

Ernesto, Quintilio, beloved Raffaele –
A cigarette or an ice-cream
Could buy your caresses, outside the Termini Station.
To the conviction of your beauty I held fast
When the tortured screams

From Gestapo headquarters rang in our ears
Through the endless months of the German occupation.
Did you only recognise me
By my bitten nails, like all pederasts?

Nembutal, Mogadon, Tavar and Mictasol
Turning my urine blue –
I am old, alone. My reputation? It's invisible –
A poet, they say, for the very few
Who see, through the mists of the twentieth century,
The universal, the sun coming through.
To the journalists
I can only say, not even trying to make sense,
'My past is risible...'

The Better Portion

The husband loved early mornings.
But the wife, give or take
The twenty percent in all of us
Open to change, slept on
To a different clock, her nightgown
A rectangle of white calico
Cut from the template of darkness.

Light changed in the various rooms
But only he saw it…. Afternoons
Were their common ground – the hot infusion
Brewed at four, the casual chat
As something came to the boil
Or simmered away, depending
On who was in charge, and who not,

And which year it was. Outside
Could have been anywhere, a world
Improvised, for argument's sake,
From the barking of neighbourhood dogs
Or a car backfiring, smells
And habits, the usual bottomless wells –
But this is beside the point,

As all who are paid to listen
Could have warned him….
                              Suddenly
One evening, she talked a blue streak
From half-past eleven
To four-fifteen, then fell asleep
Like a stone disappearing into the deep.
All this comes from nowhere

He told himself, flabbergasted
And unmanned, with the working surface
Of marriage all around him
To hold on to – heart and head,
The better portion neither disputed
In all their years of breaking bread
Before she emerged, from the underworld.

Firefly

It was zigzagging along
In the dusk, when I snatched it

Out of its path of flight
Like the hand of God

Delaying it, temporarily,
Between the why and the wherefore

Of my cupped palms
That glowed, like a votive lamp

Pulsating yellow, so I knew
It was alive in there

In the attitude of prayer
I carried ahead of me

On the latening road – a principle,
A mustardseed of light

That belonged in the dance of atoms
Around me, energies

The dark released
And I, too, had a hand in.

Søren Kierkegaard

I took you north with me, Kierkegaard,
Always intending to read you. On the train
I had nine straight hours, from Florence through to Munich
In a closed compartment…. Marshalling yards
At Bologna, the north Italian plain

That seemed to stretch forever – apples, wine,
The childhood of humanity, acres of vines
And orchards blossoming with original sin
Through windows looking outwards, looking in.
I never got down to it, your grand design –

The Stages on Life's Way were watersheds
I stretched my legs at, took the air
At fabulous but earthly altitudes
Where Austrians boarded, girls with golden hair.
Serious, bookish, riding the corridors

Into Germany, scions of adult races,
These are your readership, Kierkegaard.
The ethical life, the Protestant rage
At ecstasy, bought at a station –
I never got beyond the opening page.

Kierkegaard, I can see you shake your head
In disappointment at the sons of men
From everywhere north of the Alps, a land of the dead
Your spirit inhabits, ghosting your own books –
The Sickness unto Death, The Concept of Dread.

Bavarian traffic streams through the needle's eye
Of a manmade tunnel. Almost done
Our northward journey, and the autobahn
Keeps pace with us, converging
On Munich.... What would you know of joy,

Kierkegaard, you who hated poets,
Or the million things that pass through one man's mind
In nine hours transit, all the way from Florence,
Feeding his soul on headphones,
Dreaming of women. Things you would not understand.

Night Train Through the Brenner

Why should it seem so strange
To be travelling backwards
Out of Germany, as the hours change,

With the whole of history
In reverse, the passengers sleeping
On fettered wheels, and everyone in the dark?

When we left, it was after midnight.
New Year rockets fizzling out
On the Munich streets – a litter of celebration,

Firecrackers, broken glass,
And two hundred years of revolution
Lingering, like a sulphur smell in the nostrils....

The conductor coughs in the corridor
All night long. He can have our identities
If he gives them back in the morning

Rubberstamped. Our one desire
Is to sleep in the peace
Of body heat – let no torch shine among us! –

While someone else deciphers
The moving lights from their reflections,
The true direction of time....

The Alps are not our business –
Innsbruck, Brenner, Bolzano. A roar in our ears
As we bore through tunnels –

The watersheds of Europe
Were always too cold for us. Better to dream
Of Munich with its Christmas lights

Or the mannequins of Florence,
At one of which we will certainly wake
The morning after the ages.

Towards daybreak, the sound of voices –
An unknown station. How long have we been here?
An hour? A night? Two hundred years?

Italian speech, on a megaphone
'...*Bologna, Firenze, binario tre...*'
Drifts through the darkness. Been and gone

Is Nineteen Hundred and Eighty-nine –
The heights are behind us. Early vendors
Push their steaming trolleys

Through the small hours of Day One.
Two tramps, a railwayman,
In the light of a station buffet,

Swallow their bitter portion. For an instant
Life is the same for all of us,
Bleary-eyed, at the dawn of humanity.

The Canto of Ulysses

As the eye reads, from left to right,
Ulysses' canto, what comes next,
The day, already spread like a text
On the ceiling above me, asks to be read.
Anxiety or increasing light,
Whatever wakes me, fills my head
With the oceanic billows
Of a slept-in marriage bed.

The shutters go up, like thunder,
On the street below. If the soul fed
On coffee, aromatic bread,
Niceties raised to the power of art,
We would long ago have knuckled under
To perfection, in the green heart
Of Italy, settled here,
And gone to sleep in the years.

But what was it Dante said
About ordinary life? My mind wanders
Like Ulysses, through the early sounds,
A motor starting, taps turned on,
Unravelling Penelope's skein,
Unsatisfied, for the millionth time,
With merely keeping my feet on the ground –
As if I could ever go home!

Money, like a terrible shadow,
Unsuccess and middle age,
Darken my vision of the page
I scan from memory, where it says
Women will all be widows

To the quest, neglected fathers,
Ageing, live out lonely days,
And coastlines merge with each other.

Sound of a passing train at dawn
Through Umbrian fields, of wheat and vines,
Through cloisters and bird sanctuaries,
Feeding on overhead powerlines,
Obsesses me, with the need to be gone,
Vitality, or cowardice,
The sail of Ulysses, west of the sun,
Dwindling in Ptolemaic skies.

What did you say to me last night?
'Where you go, I go....' Sleep on that
While I watch you, curled,
Uxorious, my one satisfaction
At the heart of the known world,
Stippled with Mediterranean light,
Its yellow streaks already latent
With afternoon heat, and stupefaction.

Any day now, we hand back the key
To habit, peace, stability,
The seasonal round, festivities
Of wine and cherry. Think of the fuss
Of what to take and leave behind –
Shade for the soul, our miniature trees
Of olive, oak and southern pine –
Before the seas close over us.

5

A Spider Dance on Bahnhofstrasse

It is not Nineteen Fifteen.
Lenin and Tristan Tzara,
Sitting in Zurich, at the bar,
Over coffee and newspapers, are has-beens
Shadowing world transfiguration
Through politics or benzedrine –
Figments of the imagination.

Still, as always, there is War –
And Zurich, its conscience at ease,
Launders money, launders streetcars,
Sanctions certain refugees,
Among whom, this time, no James Joyce,
Irish, three dependants,
Author, at work on *Ulysses*,

But Lithuanian, Pole and Bulgar,
Lenin's orphans, prostitutes,
Their teeth blackened to the roots,
Angling for trade in the Langstrasse stews,
And dreamy children of Tristan Tzara,
Dadaist manifestos
Tracked in their veins, on Needle Park –

And me, in Nineteen Ninety-one,
Drinking beer in the autumn sun,
Watching the drift, on Bahnhofstrasse,
Of the indestructible bourgeois class.
Should I raise my glass,
Salute them, saying 'You have won,
The century is yours...'

And break into the spider dance,
Boneless, looselimbed,
Like our dear, departed Jim
In Flunthorn cemetery, his poem
Completed, thanks to unknown hands,
A three-month visa under my heart
To neutrality, to art?

Attila József's Trains

They're pulling in, those selfsame trains,
A century later, out of the East,
From Transylvania, the Ukraine,
To the streets of Budapest.

Gypsies, sluicing themselves at pumps.
Streetwalkers, supernaturally tall
In high-heels, fit to jump
The Iron Curtain, or the Wall,

And still come down on the losing side.
Stanzas packed with human fate
Rattle in like boxcars. Marx and Freud
And Lucifer unemployed, at Teleki station,

Watch the greenhorns stepping down
Through loansharks, dealers in cocaine –
Their karmic wheel come round again,
Their first night on the town….

Attila József, switch old lines
And draft alternatives – be driver,
Stationmaster, all at once.
Your suicide gives you leverage

Over the living – third-class trains
Converging, as they did before,
Through heat and sub-Carpathian plains
On capital cities, funeral pyres

Of appetite, of desire –
And street-boys named for you, who steal
Potatoes, floursacks, anthracite fire,
Perishing under the wheels

Of a future approaching forever.
Lean on the fulcrum of your pen
A human weight, like a pointsman's lever –
Slow time down, as it pulls in again.

MacNeice's London

(for Derek Mahon)

Hexagonal tables, soundproofed in green baize,
Littered with microphones,
Ashtrays, teacups... Your element, MacNeice,
A glasswalled studio, to be alone in
With a million listeners, there beneath Portland Place

And calling all nations. Go home from your work
And listen in to the voices
Swarming inside you. Try them out on the dark,
On paper, on the walls of your flat
In Primrose Hill, on this girlfriend or that

Who shares your bed and leaves you your bachelorhood
Old as Samuel Johnson's
Wedded to London. Mother went mad
In the Old Sod, and the Celtic Twilight
Sank in the Western Approaches. Regression and flight

Were always old hat. There is only the view from the window,
Regent's Park and Marylebone
Leafless on a winter Sunday, with nothing to do,
Only yourself to look into,
Apperceptive, stoical and true,

A string of average days
That come to nothing. See them laddering past
Like London Underground, crammed with speechless faces,
Brief, platonic. What better place
Than London, to mirror the lonely self-regard

Of a stateless person? Lay your cards
On the green baize table, it is deep underground,
A bunker of civilised sound,
A BBC studio.... Thirty years dead
I see your ghost, as the Blitz carooms overhead,

Dissolve like a smoke-ring, meditative,
Classic, outside time and space,
Alone with itself, in the presence of the nations,
Well-bred, dry, the voice
Of London, speaking of lost illusions.

Burial with Your People

Mine are scattered everywhere –
But yours... On the lee side
Of Cargin Hill, a windbreak from eternity,

Wet clay, the cladding for my bones,
Unfolds itself, maternal ground
I have wandered the earth for, all my life,

A plot the size of a double bed
I lay myself down in
Tonight, unzipped, in my birthday suit.

I should never have got you talking
On any of this. 'Even there'
You whisper 'my hand will stray....'

And I feel it, creeping along my thigh
In death as in life, an earth-spirit
Working its protective magic

About me, till I yearn for the little death
Foreshadowing the greater.
Tendrils, taproots, tingling ions

Of sex and death, in the country dark –
Now, I suppose, I will never wake
To anything more than perpetual half-light

Where the rain in squalls, like Jesus Christ,
Goes waltzing on the waters
Of Lough Neagh.... Country cousins

Snooze in adjacent rooms,
Adjacent coffins, blacked out,
While we go about our natural work

Of roots and continuities,
And I hear you whisper 'How does it feel
To be buried with my people?'

For the millionth time....
                              To say 'Yes'
As once, long ago, I must have done,
Was to take the plunge into more than marriage.

Worpswede

The black essence of the bogs,
Black sails, black metal barges
Running before the wind
On steelgrey rivers, that freeze in winter
Draining the dark hinterlands
We live in, coming together
Somewhere beyond the horizon
Where the sea is, and the cities,
Seeps into us...
                        Black ooze
In winter ploughland, and the trees
A dark roar, a windbreak
From Siberia, quarrelsome with birds,
Explosions of black crows
Cacophonous, are petrified forests,
Ghosts of themselves
Already, dissolving
In the distance, in the grey air

That is almost water. Drown in it
Like melancholy, linger and dwell
Like spirits, in the solid world
Of iron sidings, the end of the line,
Where the carbon sheets are all worked out,
The flatcars rust, the boys with no shoes
Long dead, and the railroad crews,
Are a memory.
                        Three months on,
I script us into the landscape –
Peatsmoke, the grey wash of skies
Blown over. Everything changes,
Only the mood is the same.

One of the states of the soul
Has taken root in us –
Black essence, worked like grime,
Ineradicable, in the lifelines
Of our joined hands.
We seem to have lived here forever.

Friesian Herds

Among the bulrushes, and the blackened clumps of nettles,
Marsh-marigolds, sorrels, flecks of yellow
In a green weft, the slow drift of cattle
Browsing, nibbles away at the back of my mind.
Now, in the autumn, with the ground mists
Rising around them, watered and fed,
Instinctively tired, they lie down to rest.
Their light is an orange sunspot, miles to the west.

And I clear a space for them, in the great memory –
A few flat acres, and the wraiths of trees
In the grey of oncoming rain,
And lapwings, with their otherworldly cries
Of disenchantment, endlessly shifting their ground
Like metaphysicians, breaking the peace
That was before the beginning, and will be after the end –
A few flat acres, on the north German plain,

Strung with electric fences, voltage pulsing
With the rhythm of the human heart,
Spasmodic, violent. That, and nothing else
Is what confines them. Their mottled blacks and whites
Woven, like eschatology, in the fabric of art,
The old Dutch masters, are false to them in the end,
The blobs in the background
Tugging at feedracks, drinking their fill from artesian wells

In theological innocence. Were I the God
They stumble towards, drooling cud,
The cloven-hooved, in their mulch and clabber world,
I would exempt them from biblical evil
Flooding the mudflats, and the windswept polder country,

When the plug is finally pulled
Around Cuxhaven, and the dykes implode.
I would let them go on grazing, below sea-level.

To the Korean Composer Song-On Cho

Tell me please, what all this means to you –
Thirteen years in the west, the German night
Trembling the windows of your studio
As haulage thunders past, and the Hohenzollern Ring
Adazzle with traffic, the roar of Cologne,
Sex cinemas and drugstores, supermarket lights,
Dwindle, inside you, to a Buddhist drone.
Lay it all out between us, like the tea you bring

On a china service. Bass clefs, ideograms
Litter the floorspace. Peremptory, inquisitive,
Leaping from chair to chair,
Inspecting titles 'Clock, Toy Soldier and Drum
For the Leipzig Ensemble...' hardly believing my ears
At static buzz in the room,
Tinnitus, or the music of the spheres,
I ask you – is this how an Asian woman lives,

Alone, in our midst? Instead of explanations
Listen, you bid me 'The Stronger, the Weaker Brother'
Confucian, scored for the voice
Of an ancient woman. *Once, a bird flew south,*
Returned in the Spring, two pumpkin seeds in its mouth,
For the stronger loss, for the weaker one increase –
But please, no moral! 'East and West...'
You smile as you change the spools, and give the knob a twist,

Fast-forwarding us to the present century.
Silence. A drum. From the audience a cough,
Embarrassed, as it waits
And hears itself, in the terrible void between notes.
I look at you, and you look back at me.

Is this how it has to sound when the line goes dead?
Drumtap, processional shuffle
At the court of the last boy-king, long since beheaded.

Flip the switches, plunge us back into silence,
Real, contemporary. The tea goes cold
Between us, and I watch you, as night deepens,
Listening out, for the gangs on the stairs
Who crowd your lovemaking, damn you for your laughter,
Rifle your garbage, cut your electric wires
And send you hate-mail the morning after.
'Now I can only write for the pain threshold...'

You say, as if no one is here. 'Subliminal sighs,
A waterdrop, the tick of a clock,
Or screeching kilohertz – but nothing in between.'
In the corridor footsteps, detonating through the apartment block
Like an echo chamber, bring the fear to your eyes
Till they die away, and the noise of Cologne
Takes over again, the razzmatazz
In a sonic void, where each of us is alone.

Trains East, 1991

1 *Leipzig to Dresden*

The pressurised earth is letting off steam
And the stopcocks are all open
As the train pulls out of Leipzig. Whitened fields,
A freezing brightness of snow
In azure space, and the traffic streaming through –
The western energies. Caught in the open
Hares mope, and a gang of feeding crows
Close in, on ground too freshly broken.
Where are the spectres, Chemnitz, Bitterfeld,
Legend already, and the witches brew
From the smokestacks, and the nineteenth-century dream
Of Karl Marx? Barred, off-limits, kept from sight,
Before us, behind us, to left and to right,
In the carriage beside us. In the realm of the unspoken.

2 *Frau Lang*

What will we ever know about Frau Lang,
That courteous woman, with a room to let
In the Dresden suburbs? We stayed a night
In passing, among drapes and hangings,
A turn of the century gloom
Unchanged through Hitler, Stalin. Dissident books
Lined the shelves. In the morning, in our room,
We breakfasted like Thomas Buddenbrooks
At a polished table. Fractured light and shadow
Crazily paved us, through the glazed Art Deco.
Somewhere she hovered. Divorcée or widow?
Victim? Oppressor? We could not agree.
We thanked her, handed back our skeleton key,
And left to explore the bombed reality.

3 *Gorges of the Elbe*

History runs through them now like a train –
Bad Schandau, Pirna, old spa towns,
Half-timbered houses, impossibly run down,
Sanatoria, coming to life again
After half a century. Gorges of the Elbe,
Striated rock, are the tunnels we plunge into,
Trapped in the corridor, jammed against the windows
As the drunkards pass, so full of themselves
And their new abandon. Freedom without joy –
Children of police states, out to play,
Rampaging, on the loose. And now for Prague,
Its breakable streetlamps, elegant yellow baroque,
A brawling-ground, an all-night bar
With frightened waiters, where our money goes too far.

4 *Strelnica*

The tram seems to move by itself, as it changes gear
And clatters though the empty streets of Prague
In the small hours. Another New Year!
The fake euphoria burns itself out, and the dark
Is old, directionless. We are all going home
Wherever that is. Necessity, not love,
Is telling us where to get off
At Strelnica, Ládví – wastelands, heaps of slag.
Greatcoated soldiers, out on the tear
With nothing to fight for, women with Russian parkas,
Me, without a penny to my name.
Blissed-out, happy, the worse for drink,
Only the young Czech girl has something to spare
As she leans on her lover's shoulder, and tips me the wink.

The streamlined eating-space, in the restaurant car –
As good a place as any to sit down,
Eat a homemade sandwich. 'This was a border town
In the old days....' She ventures in practised English,
Senior citizen, formerly DDR,
A nobody, in the limelights of the bar,
The bistro odours. 'For my hips, my chest,
The State has guaranteed me four weeks rest,
Electrolysis, baths, organic dishes
Free in Duisburg....' Helmstedt slides astern,
The east is behind us. 'Not that I wouldn't return,
I, whose life was ruined by the War,
Who died, so many years ago, in the flesh,
To the city of shared suffering, where my friends are.'

The Nihilists

First they were only noise in the next room
And chaos approaching. Then, they were admitted –
Acquaintances, you might say, of the third degree
And the lower depths, though swallowtailed, tophatted,
Much as we were ourselves. 'I disagree!'
They were already shouting, even among each other,
'A hundred million heads? Too high a price
To bring about, on the corpses of our fathers,
The certainty of an earthly paradise?'
I sat them down as usual, ordered tea,
And let the eternal argument resume

I first had heard in Eighteen Sixty-seven.
Old nobility, flirting with the New
In Petersburg, so many years ago,
I shuddered to remember monies given
Into the secret coffers of God knows who.
Then, I was undecided. Now, I knew.
The best I could hope for was to clear my throat
And get a word in edgeways, waste a quote
On these poor *raznochinetsi* – sneers, contempt –
In French or German, Voltaire, Diderot,
The laughable ghosts of the Enlightenment

They had done away with. 'Did you know'
A girl began deliberately, as she pared
Her fingernails, in the best modern manner,
Onto my drawingroom carpet, looked me through –
Her insolent blue spectacles, cropped hair –
'Mrs Terentyev has taken a lover –
No, I should not say lover, but a friend –
And left her husband, dead of a broken heart.

Together with Miss Varetz, they will go
In the name of rational happiness, to start
A commune in the Petersburg East End.'

Another sat at the piano, vamped a waltz
To keep the streets in ignorance outside.
I realised a thousand years had died
While I, and people like me everywhere,
Pretended interest in the Social Question,
Toured our estates, exchanged hot air
On cholera, cattle plague and good digestion,
Brought our ladies round with smelling salts
To face domestic boredom, puerperal fever,
Childbirth or miscarriage once a year,
A nineteenth-century waltz going on forever....

Yes, we were guilty. Vast allodial lands
And forests that we never should have sold,
And families of serfs we lost at cards,
Our faked returns, our traffic in dead souls –
In Switzerland, Siberia, they planned
And theorised on Ireland, Italy –
Backward too, but advanced in misery –
And never doubted that the day would come
To return from exile, at a word
Unleash millennial forces, put to flame
Countries of wooden houses, all the same.

'Give us the money for a printing press
And we'll let you be – ' Who put them up to it?
A divinity student in tarred peasant boots
Slurped from his saucer. Trembling like a leaf
A boy consumptive – feverish, glittering eyes –
Crepitated blood in his handkerchief.
I asked myself again *If this is youth*...

Another hundred years would have to pass
While they construcd, from my noncommittal smile,
Rearguard wars and massacres. Meanwhile,
The lie I lived was better than the truth.

The Ice Wager

Snowscape. Shod in tailor's irons,
Red-hot, with my poundage of weights,
I test the ice of our latest year.
Half the world is out on skates

And the other half watches. Avercamp
Or Brueghel bring the wild duck
Out of the skies, and crowd the river
With yellow leggings, anoraks,

Tobogganing children, and those dogs
More loved around here than people –
The blind or the lonely. Winter trees
Turn gelid in the freezing fog,

The roads are churned to slushy meal
By the horses. Zigzags, figures of eight
Complete the picture. But it is real,
Our wager, so place your bet

With the notary on the bank,
Impartial witness. Hollow rumblings
Out on the ice – the iron quoits,
The games in progress. Will it crumble,

Our little world, or will it hold?
Upriver from the Netherlands'
Oceangoing space, a man skates in,
A traveller, his clasped hands

Behind his back, his earflaps
Dangling. Has it fallen through,
Our worldview? But he brings no news.
Our mulled wine, our potato schnapps

Are all that concern him. Hurdy-gurdies,
Monkey dances. The Good, the True
Are beyond him, where he is travelling to.
It is down, again, to me and you,

Tonight, when I come off the ice
Which, needless to say, has never cracked
In centuries of changing skies,
To carry out the mandatory acts,

Traditional, for the time of year –
Banquets where the loser pays,
White tablecloths for the ice-floes
Junketing on, in hope and fear.

The Lap of Plenty

Leave to poets a moment of happiness
Or your world will perish

CZESŁAW MIŁOSZ

Slowly, under rain, the land is turning green,
Our land of cockaigne, of fullcorn bread
And apple wine for the asking. Cattle-sheds
Pour cattle into the fields
Of Lower Saxony. Their bellowings
Celebrate freedom, and the promise of rich yields.

A stream of yellow stale.... A horse harrumphs
In the middle distance, tears
At a cartwheel of fodder. And the last guns
Of the hunting season
Die away, as fashion parades of pheasants,
Gorgeous in mating dress, tails like electric wires,

Sashay out of hiding.... Eden before the Word!
To look is to eat, theologies
Hover in abeyance. Only this mesh of birdsong
Settling, invisibly,
Deadening thought. Let the grained wood
Of our bedroom ceiling, the patterns ecstasy wrought,

The knots, the grains of wood, be enough for once.
Let the stillness of afternoons
Lie lightly upon us. Soon we lose our place
In the scheme of ignorance,
Brueghel's barnyard, paradise of fools.
The best the earth can offer, on any given day,

Is slipping away. The letter, the telephone
Wait in the hallway.
Military trains, as they roar through the dark
Of northern Germany, bring on Kingdom Come.
Adam's curse, the need for work,
Banishes us, adaptable pair, from what was never home.

6

When the Promised Day Arrives

One golden day the whole of life contains
HÖLDERLIN

When the promised day arrives
That prophets and old wives
Are always predicting, examine your hands
Where the fatelines have been read
And what you wanted to hear is said –
At last you will understand.

The traffic, birds, pneumatic drills
Of an absolute city
Will be yours. White architecture,
Classical, and the sky a brilliant blue
In early winter, season of clarity,
Urban trains, their clean electric smell –
And the rest will be up to you

To do with as you please.
Ideal objects, the people, the trees,
Giving themselves unconsciously,
Fish and vegetable stalls, a splash of awnings
Everywhere, tobacco and coffee
Of student cafes, and the energies
Of expectation, for it is still morning

And the best is still to come.
The sizzle of meat
On skillets, Chantilly and rum
In sawdust joints, where the officeworkers eat,
The prisoners of time.
And feeling it in you, the appetite

Afterwards, someone at any price –
Her sallow skin, her almond eyes,
Black hair, and cold professional zeal
Conducting you towards release,
The old regressive peace
That was always better imagined than real,

Always unreachable…. Follow your own arc
Into decline, not all at once
But gradually. Battered shopfronts,
The immigrant quarter, littered with orange-peel,
Syringes, a ferris wheel
Stopped dead, your alter egos
Lounging at every corner, out of work,

Who dreamt, like you, of life in the ideal city.
You will take it all in
As expected; the golden afternoon,
The parks, the changing angle of light
On nave and transept, human futures and pasts.
You are not the first, you will not be the last

To follow your own shadow
As it lengthens. Dispassionate,
Steady your gaze. Already, it is late,
And the blue deepens, merciless and clear.
The unities fall into place.
Disillusionments, lost years

Are part of the story. The rest is praise –
Be equal to it, pay your way
With the same blank cheque that floats so many lives,
Your birthright and your crossing fee
When the promised day arrives.

The Garden

It was a closed space. From the moment I saw it
I knew I could depend on it.
To hell with the endless weathers
Passing above, and the high apartments
Shadowing it. Down here
On the stone bench, of an autumn morning,
I felt for a moment, the heat of sun on my face
As it angled around the corner
Out of sight. My patch of sky
Went blue then, or grey,
And I went inside.
                            But it was always there,
The garden. At its centre
A tree, a plum tree
As I discovered, when the bluish fruit
Appeared through the leaves in September,
Gave it core, and strength, and definition.
Yellow courgettes, and ripening tomatoes
Bound to their splints. And tough carnations
Half in love with the wire that fenced them in.
And the clay, of course, rich and black
After rain, or a dry brown bath
For thrushes and sparrows.
And day after day, the same man
Clearing weeds, or laying a path
According to some unspecified plan.

No need to mention where all this was.
I had travelled enough, by then,
To dispense with where. Sufficient to say
A horse's tail appeared, one day,
Above a gable, or a streak of cirrus –
Time and the future, far away.

121

Woodsmoke, the waft of cooking,
Brought me back to earth –
I was here, in the garden. An old woman
With green fingers, fed me generic names
Like Flower, or Tree,
As if nothing else mattered
But the garden, and having your own key.

God in France

To be God in France, where no one believes anymore.
To have no calls, to sit all day in cafés...

JEWISH PROVERB

Allah of Islam! Yahweh of the Jews!
   They were calling upon me
All over Paris. Sabbaths, but the Bon Dieu
Had gone missing. I had set myself free
From Friday at the mosque, that pile of shoes,
Those thousands praying, Saturday Torah scrolls
And lit menorahs, Sundays salvaging souls –
From Daubenton, Des Rosiers, Saint Gervais,
To live again in the body, *l'homme moyen sensuel*

Adrift on the everyday. Streetlife, glass cafés
   Were my chosen ground.
Whatever I needed easily could be found
In a few square miles. Massage, phlebotomy,
Thalassal brines and hydrotherapeutics,
Mont Saint Genevieve with its hermeneutics,
Clichy for hardcore, all the highs and lows
Of pure *bien-être*, like a bird in the hand.
Oh yes, if I wanted a woman, I knew where to go –

And who could deny me? Human, all my horizons
   Were reachable by train
From Austerlitz, Saint Lazare, the Gare de Lyon –
Not that I needed them. Gifted like Urizen
With omnipresence, simultaneity,
I could sit here over dinner, and still see
Normandy's apple-belt, or the lightwaves of the South
Collapsing on beaches. None could deny me
The springtime glitter of shad in the rivermouth

Of the long Garonne – that exquisite flesh,
  The bone that sticks in the throats
Of twenty centuries. Ichthyus the fish,
Like Renan's Christ, was dying, dying out
In the boredom of villages, of Proustian spires,
Provincial time, the echo-sounding fleets
Off La Rochelle, the sleep of the Loire,
The happiness that is almost too complete,
The Sunday afternoons that run on Michelin tyres.

Was that terrible? Tell me, was that sad?
  The night of the gods,
Of absences, abscondings, abdications?
Was I to kneel before him, the tramp at the station,
Unpeel his stinking trainers, wash his feet,
Amaze the wage-slaves? In the name of what
Would I drive the midnight circle of philosophers
Out of their TV studios, swivel chairs,
With hempen fire, the rope of castigation?

No, instead I would sit here, I would wait –
  A dinner, a *café crème*,
A chaser of grog. Whatever else, there was time –
Let Judgement take care of itself. To celebrate –
That was the one imperative. Randomness, flux,
Drew themselves about me as I ate,
Protected by the nearnesses of women, their sex
Blown sheer through summer dresses, loving my food,
My freedom, as they say a man should.

The Zone

Gare de l'Est…another nightmare station
   On the North-South line
Where it is always midnight, or a vision
Of down-and-outs asleep in their own moonshine.
Change for the other Paris, lower depths
Of Gare du Nord, of Jaurès, Stalingrad,
Where the addicts sleep, and the platforms are unswept,
And the cheapest heroin is always to be had,

And the line runs clear, through Laumière and Ourcq
   Past the old slaughterhouse
And the immigrant quarter, sure as a learning curve
Or the crescent of Islam, purifying as it goes
From West to East. Mohammedans descend,
Mohammedans enter. Here, you are out on your own,
A stranger from the realm of means and ends,
Cartesian ego, barrelling under the Zone

Past Porte de Pantin, through to Bobigny.
   Not that there's anything there –
The end of the line. A flight of metal stairs,
Surveillance cameras, walkways through the trees,
Political theatre, people at a bar
Between the acts, a bell about to ring,
Reminding them, discreetly, who they are,
And that they will have to answer for everything.

Mort Feldman

At the threshold of inaudibility,
You, with your hushed subliminal chords,
Me, with my onomatopoeic Word
Are two in a million. Dark at half past three –
That far-off winter when the cattle froze
In attitudes of listening, I remember
For ice and silence, all the depressive lows
You led me through. Now, in another November,
Another city, everything to prove
And nothing started, daydreaming in bed,
I think of your slow-grown fame, already dead,
A posthumous roar that drowns out New York City
With the music of inaudibility
Cattle hearken to. Trapped in a groove,
Attacking myself for failures in love, in art,
Might I from your quietness take heart,
Your still, small voice, that called the bluff
Of multitudes, and never raised the roof?

A Vision of Hokkaido in the Rain

*A Japanese Christian sect believes Christ visited
the country in his unrecorded years*

It is very quiet here, in the north of Japan,
Where everyone has forsaken me. The street
Is rain-black, drizzled, and it seems to be winter,
Probably late at night. My second coming,

Unannounced, past any civilised hour,
Is still too soon for redemption. Dark before dawn –
The market closed, the basins for live eels
Stacked neatly. One old woman in black

Squatting under the light of a low-watt bulb
Spoons noodles into herself. Do the old, I wonder,
Go as they always went here – to the boneyard
Deep in the mountains, in the inhuman cold,

And die back into their lines of ancestry?
Laughter behind closed doors, through the masking tape
Of broken, bandaged windows, in the geisha parlour –
Canned American laughter on TV.

Perhaps they are sleeping, though, the guiltless women,
Their clients gone – oblivious on sake,
Screen still running. Slide them back, the panels –
Earthly paradise! I have foreshadowed it all,

Of course, from the other side of time,
Now here I am. A *tuk-tuk* through the small hours
Sheds its wake of sparks in a neighbouring street
(If everyone were suddenly to awaken...)

And the elephants, asleep in chains
Outside the sawmill, dream in time and motion,
Hauling logs. A whiff of stinking hides –
So this is a town that lives off tannery, then,

And entertains itself, like a million others,
Eating, having sex and watching soaps.
And to speak of evil, as the rain drifts down
Past the naked bulbs of the marketplace

Left on all night, is to know redundancy
Under another wisdom, a different kind of law
Than the one that brought me north, so long ago,
In my lost, apocryphal years

Between the carpenter's shop and the death on the cross.
Perhaps no more was needed. Had I stayed
And intermarried, God alone would have known
And everyone could have slept to the end of time.

Cloudberry

Mist and blanket bog, where the ice sheets vanished.
But it is here, according to the books,
Cloudberry is to be found –
In a single patch, on the west face of Dart Mountain.
I can see you looking at me
As if to say 'What? In this weather?
Are rosehips, reddening haws and deadly nightshade
Not enough for you? Poisons, panaceas
Bursting from the hedges
Of half the country?'

Call it bakeapple, for all I care,
As the Canadians do. Alps and tundras,
Bogs and blasted heaths, are its chosen ground.
As for me, I'm tired of life reduced
To a household metaphor....
                              I want to go back
Just once, behind all that is Ireland,
To the age of free migrations
Where a man sets out, with only a Word in his head
And the needle of a shattered compass
Guiding him, through what is now no more than landscape,
With its huddle of frightened sheep
In driving westerlies, blown bog-cotton
Trembling like the beards of a million prophets
Leading their chosen peoples out of exile –
To eat of the tasteless fruit
Of universality, rooted
Like myself, in the invisible,
And belonging everywhere.

A Gulf Stream Ode

Laura Allende 1907–1984

To the west of us, like an untold epic,
Huge and silent, written in air and water,
Nutrient salts, cold-walls and foggy banks
Dissolving in each other, threading their ways
Between the islands, Bofin, Inishturk,
And the crooked nine-mile fjord of Killary Harbour,
Wittgenstein's cottage, Ownie King's post office,
Faherty's, around our summer home,
The Gulf Stream ran through childhood.
                                        High inland
I stopped a minute. For it was lifting,
That eternal mist, that blots out everything
To a distance of ten yards – a mist off the sea
I could conjure out of nowhere, to this very day,
Shrinking the world to microcosm. Waterdrops,
Fern-leaves. Squirming under my boot,
A hook in its gullet, the death-entanglements
Of a Sargasso eel. It was lifting,
And the distances, the space of pure imagining
Beyond the merely great-in-the-particular
Cleared like a depth of field. Away to the west
Were Carney's acres and his lazybeds,
Mullaghglass headland, with its burial-ground
Abutting on nothingness. Faraway no-sound –
Ocean breakers, cresting along their lengths.
And the rest a legend, as yet to be pieced together.

Yes indeed, we were an extraordinary family –
Granny Allende, our maternal ancestor,
Arucanian cheekbones, almost local,

With another life in London, summering here,
Our great enigma. How, I was asking myself
Even then, infledged at twelve or thirteen –
How had we fetched up here, in this maritime state
Of 'warm wet winters, summers cool and damp'
Our house so filled with pebbles, sea-shells, bird-cries,
Hurricane-lamps, that threw gigantic shadows,
Calcified fishes, drifted tropical seeds
Inscrutable with oceanic force
The Gulf Stream brought us? Shadows, Granny Allende –
Even then, I was spooked by my own lost origins.
Not that it mattered here, if anywhere.
Wittgenstein, they said, was a very strange man.
And Slippey Faherty, with a hook for a hand,
Salting, smoking, curing in his shed
Horse-mackerel for the winter, cod and Pollack.
Major Plaistow, back from Japanese camps,
Shacked up with a local girl. And Nora Burke
Abandoned by her man, on their wedding-night,
Who farmed the land alone.
                              In my mind's eye
I could see her down there, swishing her great scythe
Through late July. I could see them all,
Inhabitants of the Gulf Stream, local, small,
Absorbed in their business. Ownie King
With his sheepdrops and his week-old telegrams,
Eavesdropping on Greenland and the late summer run,
The Irminger, the Humboldt, Norway currents,
Awaiting a poacher's moon. Again it would fall,
The north Atlantic mist, the long depression
Stretching to the Arctic. Blow-ins, storms,
Boreal darkness, night-time closing in.
I would deny everything. Whole decades would pass.

Meanwhile though, unkillable in the grass –
Granny Allende, where on earth did you come from? –
An eel was writhing. Instinct told me
Let the thing go. Coldblooded, let it melt
In its own element, an elver-memory,
Pure nacelle, of absolute otherwhere,
Epic or legend, to get back to once again.

After Ireland

I had three delights –
Nature, books
And the bodies of women.

Let that be enough,
The hermit says,
Enough and then some.

Already we are forgetting
The essentials. Food
And warmth in winter,

For this, remember,
Is Ireland. Sky-life,
Soul-life, they come after,

With the passing of things.
But listen –
In the distance, cars,

That dark mechanical roar,
And the calligraphy
Of vapour trails in air,

And the notion of heaven,
Of retribution,
Melting, like exhaust fumes,

In desecrated space.
To be on earth,
In Ireland. The nicotine

Of a woman's kiss,
Narcotic.
The chassis in the bog,

The broken axle. Sloe-berries
In autumn, whiskey
In winter, deer returning

To dark re-forested hills.
Selfconsciousness
Without God. A solitude,

A self-sufficiency
Feeding, not on roots,
But the dream of roots.

The Bird Haunt

They had changed their throats and had the throats of birds

W.B. YEATS

Soon enough, they will come to me,
The birds, as I hunker here
In a wooden blind, on the shores of Lough Neagh,
Alone and cold, but never lonely.
All the souls will come to me,

Their given names changed
To Mallard, Moorhen, Mandarin, Merganser,
Chooking in among the reeds
Or a blatter of wings on the water
Of an absolute take-off.

Half the world has gone south –
It's winter now. Self-insulated,
Deathless, last of the early Irish hermits,
I lift the hatch like a desktop
And light floods in,

A giant scriptorium,
Sky and water. Antrim to the east,
Its reef of lights. And the dot-dash-dot
Of a pollan-fleet, on the far horizon.
And the planes, the trajectories,

Flickering endlessly in and out
Of Aldergrove airport.
An hour from now, it will be dark
And arctic. November –
The month of the long south-westerlies

And conning the lists of the dead.
Brent Goose, Whooper,
Seagull, Diver, even a notional Grebe,
Their high, piping cries
Barely audible

In the uproar of the world.
On a carpet of blackened leaves
I blew in here. And now, suspended,
My mind amphibious
Between two elements,

With the dry cough of the wildfowlers' guns
In my ears, they return to me,
Desmond, Johnny, Michael, Margaret, Charles –
Crossed over, gone but still watched for,
Dark against the water.

The Mystic Marriage

The fountain is stopped now
That made its water-noise
Into the small hours. Years ago
You thought it was rain,

Now, you sleep though everything
With the window open –
Late night jazz, a couple quarrelling,
Headlights, one mosquito.

'It is three o'clock
In the morning. I am going
To the lovers' bridge
In white mist, without you...'

I wake from that dream
Towards daybreak. You beside me
Still sleeping.
You were never a dawn person.

The fountain is on again.
Whole years have passed. And still
We have never left the south –
From where, if ever, each returns

Eternally changed, or not at all.
A white noise of swifts
Outside. Swallows sipping
Old dregs of misery –

The drained glass on the wooden table
Slowly filling with light.
And suddenly, a crash of bells
From Saint John of Malta

Hard by, and two flights down,
Approaching, lifting the spell,
A river of children's voices
Growing and growing, out of the future,

Pure annunciation. Just in time
Like a dream transcript, I retrieve it –
Our mystic marriage. Something, at last,
Has earthed itself inside you.

Benjamin Fondane Departs for the East

Look at us now, from the vanished years –
   Paris between the wars.
Penelopes and Juliets, pimps and racketeers
Of sugar and tobacco. Boys and girls
With stars on their lapels, who sleep on straw
Like everyone else, and carry out the slops.
And who could deny we're equals, under a Law
Annihilating us all? Conformists, resisters,
You I would never abandon, my own soul-sister,
Drinking brassy water from the taps

Of Drancy, where time and space are the antechamber
   To our latest idea of eternity –
Trains going east in convoys, sealed and numbered,
To an unknown destination. *Pitchipoi*
As the wits describe it, after the Yiddish tale –
A village in a clearing, zlotys changed for francs,
Children at their books, the old and frail
Looked after, and the rest suspiciously blank
On the postcards drifting like dead leaves
Back from that other world we are asked to believe in.

Death is not absolute! Two and two make five!
   My poems will survive!
Why not fly in the face of reason and scream
As Shestov says? Unscramble the anagram
Of my real name, which now is mud,
And tell Jean Wahl and Bachelard, *bien pensants*,
I forgive them, as they stalk the corridors
Of the Sorbonne, and the pages of the *Cahiers du Sud*.
I forgive us all, for we know not who we are –
Irrational, fleeting, caught between war and war,

Faking our own death, in umpteen nation-states,
    As the monies collapse
And the borders, and we all transmigrate
Like souls, through the neutral space on the map.
Athens and Jerusalem, Ulysses and the Wandering Jew –
There we all go, the living and the dead
The one in the other…call us the Paris crowd,
Unreal, uprooted, spectres drifting through,
The ashes of our ancestors in suitcases,
Bound for Buenos Aires, bound for the New.

In the steamroom dissipating, the bathhouse stink,
    As the People of the Book
Undressed themselves, I learned at last how to think.
I saw the shame and beauty, and I shook
At patriarchs' aged knees, the love-handles of hips
And women's breasts, emerging, disappearing,
Standing, kneeling, waiting, finally stripped
Of civilisation – in their natural state.
At the heart of the orgy, I saw into the years
Beyond steam and faucets, to the real Apocalypse.

And now they tell me 'Hide your poems, wait –
    Somewhere in Nineteen Eighty
Readers will find you….' I see a Paris street,
Old letterbox, a drop-zone for the infinite
In a leaf-littered hallway, where a publisher long ago
Went out of business, and a young man searches
In the sibylline mess and the overflow
For a few lost words – *my own soul-sister, my wife*
Till death us do part, in the Eastern Marches…
And that, who knows, will be an afterlife.

ACKNOWLEDGEMENTS

The editors gratefully acknowledge permission to use poems in this volume from the following:

From *The Walls of Carthage* (1977): 'Blue',* 'North Wall', 'Blue Room', 'Morning', 'Metempsychosis', and 'The Walls of Carthage'.*

From *Office of the Salt Merchant* (1979): 'Middle C', 'Office of the Salt Merchant',* 'The Desert Route',* 'Latitude 5°N',* 'Loneliness in the Tropics',* 'Plague and Hospice',* 'The Niger Ferry', and 'Government Quarters'.*

From *Comparative Lives* (1982): 'Michael Praetorius', 'The Family Bass', 'Military Presence, Cobh 1899',* 'Calf Love', 'Indian Sequence', 'Monsoon Girl',* 'The Seamstress',* 'Death of Thomas Merton',* and 'The Holding Centre'.

From *The Liberal Cage* (1988): 'Dag Hammarskjöld', 'Euclid Avenue', 'The Angel', 'The Waking Hour', 'Early Christians', 'Vaucluse', and 'Eccles Street, Bloomsday 1982'.*

* Reprinted in *The Desert Route: Selected Poems* 1973-1988 (1992).

From *Night Train Through the Brenner* (1994): 'Exiles', 'In Earthquake Country', 'The River', 'At the Grave of Silone', 'Taking the Waters', 'The Poet Sandro Penna, in Old Age', 'The Better Portion', 'Firefly', 'Søren Kierkegaard', 'Night Train through the Brenner', 'The Canto of Ulysses', and 'The Nihilists' used with permission of the author and The Gallery Press.

'Conversations by the Hudson', 'A Spider Dance on the Bahnhofstrasse', 'Attila József's Trains', 'MacNeice's London', 'Burial with your People', 'Worpswede', 'Friesian Herds', 'To the Korean Composer Song-On Cho', 'Trains East, 1991', 'The Ice', 'Wager', and 'The Lap of Plenty' used with permission of the author.

'When the Promised Day Arrives', 'The Garden', 'God in France', 'The Zone', 'Mort Feldman', 'A Vision of Hokkaido in the Rain', 'Cloudberry', 'A Gulf Stream Ode', 'After Ireland', 'The Bird-Haunt', 'The Mystic Marriage', 'Benjamin Fondane Departs for the East' from *Secular Eden: Paris Notebooks 1994-2004*, used with permission of the author and Wake Forest University Press.